Valentine's Day
in the
Federal Courts

edited by
JOSHUA WARREN

This is a study of "Valentine's Day" in the opinions of the U.S. Federal Courts. All of the cases cited are U.S. Federal Court opinions that include the phrase Valentine's Day. Words and phrases that are near "Valentine's Day" in those court opinions are arranged here, out of context, to become a word cloud with footnotes. This cut-up analysis explores the cultural associations of Valentine's Day and is itself a surrealist love poem intended as a Valentine's Day gift for law lovers.

This study reveals a romantic holiday and an important business season but it is also a dangerous time of sexual uncertainties and overconsumption. Note the contradictions of a secularized-religious holiday and as sexualized-public holiday. The crossed markets of flowers, candy, and jewelry lead to turmoil in families, schools, and workplaces.

"She knew that he loved her.
She even heard on Valentine's Day that things were going great with them."

Rivero v. McNeil,
2010 U.S. Dist. LEXIS 6706
(S.D. Fla., Jan. 7, 2010)

VALENTINE'S DAY
in the FEDERAL COURTS

"Valentine's Day is a curious blend of a religious holiday"[1], "the religious origin of Valentine's Day can only be characterized as remote"[2], "Valentine's Day does have a certain degree of secular (and commercial) significance"[3], "American culture and commercialism"[4]

"various holidays along the line"[5], "Among these holidays are included Christmas, Easter, Passover, Hannukah, St. Valentine's Day, St. Patrick's Day, Thanksgiving and Halloween"[6],

---

1 Russ Berrie & Co. v. United States, Court, 23 C.I.T. 429; 57 F. Supp. 2d 1184 (C.I.T. July 13, 1999)

2 Florey v. Sioux Falls School Dist., 619 F.2d 1311 (8th Cir. April 22, 1980)

3 Florey v. Sioux Falls School Dist., 619 F.2d 1311 (8th Cir. April 22, 1980)

4 Adil Lahrichi v. Lumera Corp., 2006 U.S. Dist. LEXIS 18556 (W.D. Wash. March 2, 2006))

5 First Nat'l Bank v. Dudley, 231 F.2d 396 (9th Cir. March 13, 1956)

6 Florey v. Sioux Falls School Dist., 619 F.2d 1311 (8th Cir., April 22, 1980); Clever v. Cherry Hill Township Bd. of Educ., 838 F. Supp. 929 (D.N.J., Dec. 2, 1993)

"associated with particular recognized holidays -- specifically, Valentine's Day, Easter, the Fourth of July, Halloween, Thanksgiving, and Christmas."[7]

"peak market periods came at certain holidays such as Valentine's Day, Easter, Mother's Day, and Christmas."[8]
"demand for ferns is greatest around the Valentine's Day, Easter, and Mother's Day holidays."[9]

"Near holidays such as Christmas, Valentine's Day, Easter and Father's Day, the mail room must process approximately three times the amount of mail received on non-holidays and this causes processing delays."[10]

---

7 Wilton Indus. v. United States, 31 C.I.T. 863; 493 F. Supp. 2d 1294 (June 11, 2007)

8 Sunnyside Nurseries v. Commissioner, 1972 U.S. Tax Ct. LEXIS 39 (Oct. 19, 1972)

9 Caro-Galvan v. Curtis Richardson, Inc., 993 F.2d 1500 (11th Cir., June 25, 1993)

10 Ashker v. Schwarzenegger, 2009 U.S. Dist. LEXIS 25092 (N.D. Cal, March 25, 2009)

"flower-buying holidays"[11],
"church bell's ringing"[12], "marriage"[13],
"wedding anniversaries"[14], "ceremony"[15],
"occasions for funerals and weddings"[16],
"Sweetest Day and her birthday"[17], "sundry
birthdays"[18], "Secretary Day/Week, D-Day,
Martin Luther King's Birthday, Good
Friday,"[19] "New Years"[20], "Memorial
Day"[21], "Fourth of July"[22], "Super Bowl"[23],

11 Asociacion Colombiana de Exportadores v. United States, Consol, 22 C.I.T. 173; 6 F. Supp. 2d 865 (March 25, 1998).

12 Lautner v. Berghuis, 694 F. Supp. 2d 698 ((W.D. Mich., Feb. 16, 2010)

13 Renfrow v. Draper, 232 F.3d 688 (9th Cir., Nov. 14, 2000)

14 Sutherland v. Islamic Republic of Iran, 151 F. Supp. 2d 27 (D.D.C., June 25, 2001)

15 Wiswall v. Tanner, 145 B.R. 672 (W.D. Wash., Sept. 30, 1992)

16 Vogel v. Trans World Airlines, 346 F. Supp. 805 (W.D. Miss., May 10, 1971).

17 Bearce v. United States, 1979 U.S. Dist. LEXIS 14748 (N.D. Ill., Jan. 30, 1979)

18 Anheuser-Busch, Inc. v. Florists Ass'n of Greater Cleveland, Inc, 603 F. Supp. 35 (N.D. Ohio, Oct. 12, 1984)

19 Minnis v. Much Shelist Freed Denenberg & Ament, P.C., 3 F. Supp. 2d 877 (N.D. Ill., March 5, 1997)

20 Popeck v. Secretary of Health & Human Servs., 1993 U.S. Claims LEXIS 196, (Jan. 12, 1993)

21 Estate of Heiser v. Islamic Republic of Iran, 466 F. Supp. 2d 229 (D.D.C, Dec. 22, 2006)

22 Sutherland v. Islamic Republic of Iran, 151 F. Supp. 2d 27 (D.D.C. June 25, 2001); Wilton Indus. v. United States, 31 C.I.T. 863; 493 F. Supp. 2d 1294 (June 11, 2007)

23 TelAmerica Media Inc. v. AMN TV, 2002 U.S. Dist. LEXIS 18360 (E.D. PA, Sept. 26, 2002); Ligotti v. Garofalo, 2008 DNH 123; 562 F. Supp. 2d 204 (D.N.H., June 26, 2008)

"Mardi Gras, and the President's Day holiday weekend"[24],
"to take the weekend off"[25], "voyage"[26],
"vacation"[27], "parade"[28],
"fund-raising dinners"[29],
"trip to a theme or amusement park"[30]

"friends and acquaintances"[31], "family gathering"[32], "family fight"[33], "family photograph"[34], "an annual family Valentine's Day scavenger hunt"[35],

24 Scurtu v. Hospitality & Catering Mgmt. Servs., 2010 U.S. Dist. LEXIS 75673 (S.D. Ala. July 27, 2010)

25 Casper v. Gunite Corp., 1999 U.S. Dist. LEXIS 13554 (N.D. Ind. June 11, 1999)

26 In re Complaint of Armatur, S.A., 710 F. Supp. 390 (D.P.R. Sept. 15, 1988)

27 Marangos v. Flarion Techs., Inc., 264 Fed. Appx. 176 (3d Cir., Feb. 13, 2008)

28 Litvinov v. Holder, 605 F.3d 548 (8th Cir., May 20, 2010)

29 United States v. Mokol, 957 F.2d 1410 (7th Cir., March 18, 1992)

30 Bedi Photographics Corp. v. Polaroid Corp., 1980 U.S. Dist. LEXIS 15629 (E.D. P.A. Aug. 11, 1980)

31 Westfield High Sch. L.I.F.E. Club v. City of Westfield, 249 F. Supp. 2d 98 (D. Mass. March 17, 2003)

32 United States v. Zauber, 857 F.2d 137 (3d Cir., Nov. 10, 1988)

33 Vance v. Warden, Hocking Corr. Facility, 2011 U.S. Dist. LEXIS 127417 (S.D. Ohio, Nov. 3, 2011)

34 Sutherland v. Islamic Republic of Iran, 151 F. Supp. 2d 27 (D.D.C., June 25, 2001)

35 Durden v. Sec'y of the HHS, 2007 U.S. Claims LEXIS 519 (Sept. 26, 2007)

"wife"[36], "girlfriend"[37], "daughter"[38], "stepdaughter"[39], "brothers"[40], "sister"[41], "grandmother"[42], "mother spoon-feeds him the dessert"[43],

36 Grove v. United States, Civ, 170 F. Supp. 176 (E.D.Va., Feb. 10, 1959); Stafford v. Missouri, 835 F. Supp. 1136 (W.D. Miss., Oct. 13, 1993); Baskerville v. Culligan Int'l Co., 50 F.3d 428, (7th Cir., March 20, 1995); Black v. Zaring Homes, 104 F.3d 822 (6th Cir., Jan. 14, 1997); Arnold v. Cockrell,2002 U.S. Dist. LEXIS 12070 (N.D.Tex., July 2, 2002; Bourbeau v. City of Chicopee, 445 F. Supp. 2d 106 (D.Mass., July 26, 2006); Tillman v. United States, 2006 U.S. Dist. LEXIS 53409 (N.D. Ill,, Aug. 2, 2006); Thompson v. Fajerstein, 2008 U.S. Dist. LEXIS 78264 (N.D. Ill, Sept. 17, 2008); Young v. Hedgpeth, 2009 U.S. Dist. LEXIS 68513 (C.D. Cal, July 6, 2009); Wade v. Warden, Lebanon Corr. Inst., 2009 U.S. Dist. LEXIS 124237 (S.D. Ohio, Nov. 10, 2009); Dintelman v. United States, 2012 U.S. Dist. LEXIS 13032 (E.D. Ark., Feb. 3, 2012); Mims v. Walsh, 2012 U.S. Dist. LEXIS 147664 (S.D.N.Y, Oct. 3, 2012); Vackar v. Sentry Supply Inc., 2013 U.S. Dist. LEXIS 94544 (S.D. Tex., July 8, 2013); Betters v. Geo Group, Inc., 2013 U.S. Dist. LEXIS 111102 (S.D. Ind., July 22, 2013); Vackar v. Sentry Supply Inc., 2014 U.S. Dist. LEXIS 147 (S.D. Tex., Jan. 2, 2014)

37 United States v. Lanham, 617 F.3d 873 (6th Cir., Aug. 24, 2010); Woolever v. Lopez, 2011 U.S. Dist. LEXIS 85393 (E.D. Cal., Aug. 2, 2011); Smith v. United States, 2011 U.S. Dist. LEXIS 60323 (S.D.N.Y., June 6, 2011); Sprunger v. Thaler, 2010 U.S. Dist. LEXIS 56678 (S.D. Tex., June 9, 2010); Webster v. Fischer, 694 F. Supp. 2d 163 (N.D.N.Y., Feb. 22, 2010); Renfro v. Adams, 2009 U.S. Dist. LEXIS 17039 (E.D. Cal., Feb. 20, 2009)

38 Langer v. Comm'r, No. T.C. Memo 2008-255 (Nov. 12, 2008, aff'd by 8th Cir, June 21, 2010); Kendall v. Vill. of Maywood, 2009 U.S. Dist. LEXIS 30917 (N.D. Ill., April 9, 2009); Bostic v. United States Capitol Police, 644 F. Supp. 2d 106 (D.D.C., Aug. 6, 2009)

39 United States v. C.R., 792 F. Supp. 2d 343 (E.D.N.Y., May 16, 2011)

40 In re Ingleside Assoc., 136 B.R. 955 (Bankr. E.D. Pa., Feb. 20, 1992); and

Lescailles v. Ann Taylor Distrib. Servs., 2007 U.S. Dist. LEXIS 68262 (W.D. Ken., Sept. 14, 2007)

41 Allen v. Senkowski, 178 F. Supp. 2d 318 (E.D.N,Y., Dec. 26, 2001)

42 Moore v. Hulick, 2008 U.S. Dist. LEXIS 6325 (C.D. Ill., Jan. 29, 2008); And

Cannedy v. Adams, 2009 U.S. Dist. LEXIS 102514 (C.D. Cal. Nov. 4, 2009) Cannedy v. Adams, 2009 U.S. Dist. LEXIS 102562 (C.D. Cal., Nov. 2, 2009)

43 Gilbert v. New Line Prods., 2009 U.S. Dist. LEXIS 130675 (C.D. Cal., Nov. 16, 2009)

"The one symbol which has become universally known to symbolize Valentine's Day is the heart"[44],

"heart shape and the color red are traditionally associated with Valentine's Day."[45]

"a red heart"[46], "pink heart"[47],
"red packaging"[48],
"heart-shaped boxes"[49],

44 Russ Berrie & Co. v. United States, 23 C.I.T. 429; 57 F. Supp. 2d 1184 (July 13, 1999)

45 Midwest of Canon Falls v. United States, Court, 20 C.I.T. 123 (Jan. 18, 1996); quoted in Russ Berrie & Co. v. United States, 23 C.I.T. 429; 57 F. Supp. 2d 1184 (July 13, 1999)

46 XXL of Ohio, Inc. v. City of Broadview Heights, 341 F. Supp. 2d 765 (N.D. Ohio, Feb. 24, 2003)

47 Russ Berrie & Co. v. United States, 23 C.I.T. 429; 57 F. Supp. 2d 1184 (July 13, 1999); quoted in Wilton Indus. v. United States, 31 C.I.T. 863; 493 F. Supp. 2d 1294 (June 11, 2007)

48 Regal Jewelry Co. v. Kingsbridge Int'l, 999 F. Supp. 477 (S.D.N.Y., March 23, 1998)

49 Wallace Int'l Silversmiths, Inc. v. Godinger Silver Art Co., 916 F.2d 76 (2d Cir., Oct. 17, 1990); Atlantic Paper Box Co. v. Whitman's Chocolates, 844 F. Supp. 1038 (E.D. Pa., Feb. 2, 1994); Banff Ltd. v. Limited, Inc., 869 F. Supp. 1103 (S.D.N.Y., Nov. 14, 1994); Hershy the Tin Man v. Avon Products Inc., 1999 U.S. Dist. LEXIS 23003 (D.Mont., July 8, 1999); Goscicki v. Custom Brass & Copper Specialities, Inc., 229 F. Supp. 2d 743 (E.D. Mich., Sept. 30, 2002); Bonazoli v. R.S.V.P. Int'l, Inc., C.A. 353 F. Supp. 2d 218 (D.R.I., Jan. 18, 2005); Tesoriero v. Syosset Cent. Sch. Dist., 382 F. Supp. 2d 387; (E.D.N.Y., Aug. 8, 2005)

"myriad of heart-shaped boxes, figures, jewelry items"[50],

"terracotta container specifically designed, marketed and sold for Valentine's Day"[51],

"market candy intended for Valentine's Day in heart-shaped boxes"[52],

"heart-shaped pen holder"[53],

"little girls in dresses with unadorned hearts on their collars"[54],

"fix his heart"[55].

50 Hershy the Tin Man v. Avon Products Inc., 1999 U.S. Dist. LEXIS 23003 (D.Mont., July 8, 1999)

51 Russ Berrie & Co. v. United States, 23 C.I.T. 429; 57 F. Supp. 2d 1184 (July 13, 1999)

52 Third Restatement of the Law, Unfair Competition, Ch. 3, Illustration 8; as quoted in Wallace Int'l Silversmiths, Inc. v. Godinger Silver Art Co, 916 F.2d 76 (2d Cir., July 16, 1990) ; Bonazoli v. R.S.V.P. Int'l, Inc., 353 F. Supp. 2d 218 (D.R.I., Jan. 18, 2005); Goscicki v. Custom Brass & Copper Specialities, Inc., 229 F. Supp. 2d 743 (E.D. Mich., Sept. 30, 2002); Banff Ltd. v. Limited, Inc., 869 F. Supp. 1103 (S.D.N.Y., Nov. 14, 1994)

53 Smith v. V.I. Port Authority, 2008 U.S. Dist. LEXIS 67737, (D.V.I., Sept. 3, 2008)

54 Samara Bros. v. Wal-Mart Stores, 165 F.3d 120 (2d Cir., Dec. 28, 1998)

55 Magill v. Precision Sys. Mfg., 2006 U.S. Dist. LEXIS 16923, (N.D.N.Y, Feb. 27, 2006)

"Valentine's Day gift"[56],

"Valentine's Day present"[57],

"romantic notion"[58], "romantic souvenir"[59],

"sentimental value"[60].

56 Palmer v. Board of Education, 466 F. Supp. 600 (N.D. Ill, Jan. 31, 1979); Cram v. Lamson & Sessions Co., 49 F.3d 466 (8th Cir., March 15, 1995); Feltner v. Partyka, 945 F. Supp. 1188 (N.D.Ind., Oct. 8, 1996); United States v. Walker, 1996 U.S. App. LEXIS 33318 (10th Cir., Dec. 20, 1996); Porchia v. Cohen, 1999 U.S. Dist. LEXIS 8239 (E.D. Pa., June 3, 1999); Russ Berrie & Co. v. United States, 23 C.I.T. 429; 57 F. Supp. 2d 1184 (July 13, 1999); Leonard v. Pepsico, Inc., 88 F. Supp. 2d 116 (S.D.N.Y., Aug. 4, 1999); Estate of Cavett v. Commissioner, T.C. Memo 2000-91 (March 15, 2000); Victoria's Secret Stores v. Artco Equip. Co., 194 F. Supp. 2d 704 (S.D. Ohio, March 27, 2002); Soliman v. Deutsche Bank AG, 2004 U.S. Dist. LEXIS 9087 (S.D.N.Y., , May 19, 2004); United States v. Payton, 405 F.3d 1168 (10th Cir., May 4, 2005); United States v. Ferryman, 444 F.3d 1183 (9th Cir., April 18, 2006); Rayfield v. David (In re David), 2008 Bankr. LEXIS 1595 (S.D. Fla., May 21, 2008); Ligotti v. Garofalo, 2008 DNH 123; 562 F. Supp. 2d 204 (June 26, 2008); Thompson v. Fajerstein, 2008 U.S. Dist. LEXIS 78264, (N.D. Ill., Sept. 17, 2008); Renfro v. Adams, 2009 U.S. Dist. LEXIS 17039 (E.D.Cal., Feb. 20, 2009); Galeski v. City of Dearborn, 690 F. Supp. 2d 603 (E.D. Mich., Jan. 27, 2010 affirmed 6th Cir. 2011);   Idy v. Holder, 674 F.3d 111 (1st Cir., March 23, 2012); Phan v. CSK Auto, Inc., (N.D. Cal., Aug. 27, 2012); Lawrence v. Marshall, 2012 U.S. Dist. LEXIS 184991 (C.D. Cal., Sept. 27, 2012); United States v. Boscarino, 2013 U.S. Dist. LEXIS 62235 (D.Az., April 29, 2013)

57 Porchia v. Cohen, 1999 U.S. Dist. LEXIS 8239 (E.D. Pa., June 3, 1999); United States v. Kelley, 2006 U.S. Dist. LEXIS 88350, (E.D. Ark., Dec. 5, 2006); Pugni v. Reader's Digest Ass'n, 2007 U.S. Dist. LEXIS 26284 (S.D.N.Y., April 5, 2007); Marshall v. NYC Bd. of Elections, 2007 U.S. Dist. LEXIS 101415 (S.D.N.Y., Aug. 16, 2007); Burleson v. Kernan, 2007 U.S. Dist. LEXIS 86964 (N.D. Cal., Nov. 15, 2007); Enriquez v. United States Cellular Corp., 2008 U.S. Dist. LEXIS 92762 (N.D Ill., Nov.14, 2008); Galeski v. City of Dearborn, 690 F. Supp. 2d 603 (D. Mich., Jan. 27, 2010 affirmed by 6th Cir.., 2011); Douglas v. Brookville Area Sch. Dist., 836 F. Supp. 2d 329 (W.D. Pa., Dec. 8, 2011); Dintelman v. United States, 2012 U.S. Dist. LEXIS 13032 (E.D.Ark., Feb., 2012)

58 An Na Huang v. Mukasey, 525 F.3d 559 (7th Cir., Feb.15, 2008)

59 United States v. Dixon, 185 F.3d 393 (5th Cir., Aug. 16, 1999)

60 Hergenroeder v. Travelers Prop. Cas. Ins. Co, 249 F.R.D. 595 (E.D. Cal., April 21, 2008)

"Valentine's Day shopping"[61],
"advertisements"[62], "take advantage of Valentine's Day business"[63],
"retailers' shelves"[64],
"florist industry"[65],
"the industry of making boxes for Valentine's Day candies"[66],
"busy jewelry season"[67],
"cash register"[68], "busy season"[69],
"100,000 roses from the bushes"[70],
"peak market"[71],
"high price times in the United States"[72]

---

61 Acosta v. United States, 2010 U.S. Dist. LEXIS 10907 (W.D. Tex., Feb. 9, 2010)

62 Lott v. J.W. O'Connor & Co., 991 F. Supp. 785 (N.D. Miss., Jan. 22, 1998)

63 In re Baum's Florist, Inc., 65 B.R. 814 (E.D. Tenn., Aug. 25, 1986)

64 American Greetings Corp. v. Easter Unlimited, Inc., 579 F. Supp. 607 (S.D.N.Y., Dec. 12, 1983)

65 Florist's Transworld Delivery v. Worldwide Flower & Gift Emporium, 1998 U.S. Dist. LEXIS 7818 (D.Nev., Jan. 26, 1998)

66 Atlantic Paper Box Co. v. Whitman's Chocolates, 844 F. Supp. 1038 (E.D. Pa., Feb. 3, 1994)

67 Small v. Clark, Case No. 2006 U.S. Dist. LEXIS 48448 (M.D. Fla. July 17, 2006)

68 Katerelos v. Commissioner, Docket, T.C. Memo 1996-340 (July 29, 1996,)

69 NLRB v. Pecheur Lozenge Co, 209 F.2d 393 (2d Cir., Dec. 31, 1953)

70 Flores de N.M., Inc. v. Banda Negra Int'l, Inc., 151 B.R. 571 (March 8, 1993)

71 Sunnyside Nurseries v. Commissioner, 59 T.C. 113 (Oct. 19, 1972); quoted in Thirup v. Commissioner, 59 T.C. 122 (Oct. 19, 1972; Endres Floral Co. v. United States, 450 F. Supp. 16 (N.D. Ohio, Nov. 18, 1977)

"niche market"[73],

"capitalize on fad promotions, capture seasonal markets"[74], "promotional offer"[75],
"peak demand periods"[76],

"prices because of high demand"[77],

"high volume sales period for perfume"[78],

"the largest volume of rose sales"[79],

"fashion shows and special exhibitions"[80],

"temporary art installation"[81],

"flowers and chocolates delivered"[82],

"designers of Valentine's Day cards would be at risk of copyright infringement"[83].

72 Floral Trade Council v. United States, 12 C.I.T. 1163; 704 F. Supp. 233 (Dec. 27, 1988)

73 Lott v. J.W. O'Connor & Co., 991 F. Supp. 785 (N.D. Miss., Jan. 23, 1998)

74 Estate of Paxton v. Commissioner, T.C. Memo 1982-464 (Aug. 9, 1982)

75 Rossario's Fine Jewelry, Inc. v. Paddock Publ'ns, Inc., 2007 U.S. Dist. LEXIS 61622 (N.D. Ill., Aug. 22, 2007)

76 Tarapore v. McNamara, 2004 U.S. Dist. LEXIS 13934 (S.D. Ind., Feb. 13, 2004)

77 Roses, Inc. v. United States, 13 C.I.T. 662; 720 F. Supp. 180 (Aug. 18, 1989)

78 Nina Ricci, S.A.R.L. v. Gemcraft, Ltd., 612 F. Supp. 1520 (S.D.N.Y., July 11, 1985)

79 Floral Trade Council v. United States, 20 C.I.T. 595 (May 17, 1996)

80 Saada v. King of Prussia Associates, 1989 U.S. Dist. LEXIS 4347 (E.D.Pa, April 18, 1989)

81 Sole v. Wyner, 551 U.S. 74; 127 S. Ct. 2188; 167 L. Ed. 2d 1069 (June 4, 2007)

82 Burrell v. City Univ. of New York, 894 F. Supp. 750 (S.D.N.Y., Aug. 17, 1995)

83 Samara Bros. v. Wal-Mart Stores, 165 F.3d 120 (2d Cir., Dec. 28, 1998)

"Hallmark's merchandise is seasonal"[84], "ship Valentine's Day merchandise the year before Valentine's Day"[85],

"Restaurant's most important day of the off-season"[86], "big Valentines Day promotion. A cake decorator was expected"[87], "multi-tiered cake"[88],

"employees were required to work"[89],

"fired on Valentine's Day"[90].

---

84 Pristine Industries, Inc. v. Hallmark Cards, Inc., 753 F. Supp. 140 (S.D.N.Y, Dec. 26, 1990)

85 Mass. Mut. Life Ins. Co. v. United States, 2012 U.S. Claims LEXIS 47 (Jan. 30, 2012)

86 Habe v. 333 Bayville Ave. Rest. Corp., 2012 U.S. Dist. LEXIS 4367 (E.D.N.Y, Jan. 13, 2012,)

87 Pierson v. Mrs. Fields Cookies, 857 F. Supp. 867 (D. Utah, July 13, 1994)

88 Wilton Indus. v. United States, 31 C.I.T. 863; 493 F. Supp. 2d 1294 (June 11, 2007)

89 Brandt v. Magnificent Quality Florals Corp., 2009 U.S. Dist. LEXIS 32079 (S.D.Fla., March 31, 2009)

90 Kokkinis v. Ivkovich, 10 F. Supp. 2d 995 (N.D. Ill., July 13, 1998)

"candy box"[91], "cookies"[92],
"give chocolates"[93], "dark chocolate"[94],
"homemade fudge"[95],
"ice cream sandwich"[96],

"SweeTarts with hearts on the package"[97],
"a piece of candy before Valentines Day in
2002 that had the words 'my babe' on it."[98]

---

91 Atlantic Paper Box Co. v. Whitman's Chocolates, 844 F. Supp. 1038 (E.D. Pa., Feb. 2, 1994); Redwine v. Astrue, 2013 U.S. Dist. LEXIS 84702, (E.D. La., May 20, 2013)

92 Pierson v. Mrs. Fields Cookies, 857 F. Supp. 867 (D. Utah, July 13, 1994); Robinson v. United States Postal Serv., 1995 U.S. Dist. LEXIS 14452 (E.D. Pa., Sept. 27, 1995); Westfield High Sch. L.I.F.E. Club v. City of Westfield, 249 F. Supp. 2d 98 (D. Mass., March 17, 2003); Seats v. Kaskaskia College Cmty. College Dist. # 501, 2008 U.S. Dist. LEXIS 100944 (S.D. Ill., Dec. 15, 2008)

93 Adil Lahrichi v. Lumera Corp., 2006 U.S. Dist. LEXIS 18556 (W.D. Wash. March 2, 2006)

94 Mitchell v. City of Pittsburgh, 2014 U.S. Dist. LEXIS 6119 (W.D. Pa., Jan. 17, 2014); Hergenroeder v. Travelers Prop. Cas. Ins. Co., 249 F.R.D. 595 (E.D. Cal., April 21, 2008) ("Dark chocolate brown standing water was on the downstairs floor")

95 Papelino v. Albany College of Pharm., 2009 U.S. Dist. LEXIS 82939 (N.D.N.Y., Sept. 11, 2009) Affirmed in part and reversed in part by, Remanded by Papelino v. Albany College of Pharm. of Union Univ., 2011 U.S. App. LEXIS 1386 (2d Cir. N.Y., Jan. 24, 2011)

96 Galeski v. City of Dearborn, 690 F. Supp. 2d 603 (E.D. Mich., Decided, Jan. 27, 2010) Aff'd by Galeski v. City of Dearborn, 2011 U.S. App. LEXIS 17067 (6th Cir. Mich., 2011)

97 Sunmark, Inc. v. Ocean Spray Cranberries, 1994 U.S. Dist. LEXIS 15186 (N.D. Ill., Oct. 13, 1994)

98 Davis v. Cumberland County, 2005 U.S. Dist. LEXIS 11782 (D. Me., June 16, 2005)

"a card, a teddy bear and chocolates in a heart shaped box."[99],

"she had seen the bear and chocolates but had been expecting roses"[100],

"note in a bouquet of Valentine's day flowers"[101],

"he sent flowers to her home"[102],

"to buy his wife flowers"[103],

"three carnations"[104],

"giving roses to her old neighbors"[105],

"anonymous gift of roses"[106],

"distributed roses to several female employees"[107]

---

99 Tesoriero v. Syosset Cent. Sch. Dist, 382 F. Supp. 2d 387 (E.D.N.Y., Aug. 8, 2005)

100 Idy v. Holder, 674 F.3d 111 (1st Cir., March 23, 2012)

101 United States v. Lentz, 282 F. Supp. 2d 399 (E.D. Va., May 14, 2002) Motion denied by United States v. Lentz, 225 F. Supp. 2d 666 (E.D. Va., 2002)

102 Mehringer v. Vill. of Bloomingdale, 2003 U.S. Dist. LEXIS 11040 (E.D. Ill., June 27, 2003)

103 Tillman v. United States, 2006 U.S. Dist. LEXIS 53409 (N.D. Ill., , Aug. 2, 2006)

104 Dawn L. v. Greater Johnstown Sch. Dist., 586 F. Supp. 2d 332 (W.D. Pa., Nov. 13, 2008)

105 Miller v. Yates, 2009 U.S. Dist. LEXIS 83885 (C.D. Cal., Aug. 11, 2009)

106 Specht v. Dalton, 1999 U.S. App. LEXIS 29795 (9th Cir., Nov. 10, 1999)

107 Publishers Printing Co. v. NLRB, 1996 U.S. App. LEXIS 33958 (6th Cir., Dec. 23, 1996,), Reported in Table Case Format at: 106 F.3d 401, 1996 U.S. App. LEXIS 41658.

"in accordance with her request,
a box of chocolates, a rose,
a Wendy's lunch and a card"[108]
"given her an expensive purse"[109],
"an expensive gold necklace"[110],
"gave the bracelet to his girlfriend"[111],
"bouquet of balloons"[112],
"baby plush toy"[113], "gave her a ring"[114],
"ruby ring"[115], "an investment-quality
diamond weighing 7-8 carats as a
Valentine's Day gift for his wife"[116],
"camera"[117], "scarf"[118],

108 United States v. Castellon, 213 Fed. Appx. 732 (10th Cir., Jan. 24, 2007)

109 United States v. Freeman, 2011 U.S. App. LEXIS 25494 (10th Cir., Dec. 21, 2011)

110 Cram v. Lamson & Sessions Co., 49 F.3d 466 (8th Cir., March 15, 1995)

111 Renfro v. Adams, 2009 U.S. Dist. LEXIS 17039 (E.D. Cal., Feb. 20, 2009)

112 Lange v. Quarterman, 2009 U.S. Dist. LEXIS 86097 (S.D. Tex., Sept. 18, 2009)

113 Aurora World, Inc. v. TY Inc., 719 F. Supp. 2d 1115 (C.D. Cal., Dec. 15, 2009)

114 Doe v. Claiborne County, 103 F.3d 495 (6th Cir., Dec. 26, 1996)

115 Nicely v. Lewis, 2008 U.S. Dist. LEXIS 24648 (E.D. Tenn., March 27, 2008)

116 Thompson v. Fajerstein, U.S. Dist. LEXIS 78264, (N.D. Ill., Sept. 17, 2008);
Motion denied by Thompson v. Fajerstein, 2009 U.S. Dist. LEXIS 10659 (N.D. Ill.,
Feb. 12, 2009)Related proceeding at Thompson v. Fajerstein (In re Fajerstein), 2010
Bankr. LEXIS 3958 (Bankr. S.D. Fla., Oct. 6, 2010)

117 Infohand Co. v. Sprint Spectrum, L.P., 2006 U.S. Dist. LEXIS 98334 (D. Kan.,
Dec. 18, 2006)

"$10 money order"[119], "gift certificates"[120], "enjoy your Valentine's Day card, ten dollars, and that one picture especially for you"[121], "pictures of himself, letters, stuffed animals for Valentine's Day, music CDs"[122], "shopping for clothes"[123],

"The Miracle Bra advertising"[124], "Victoria's Secrets gifts"[125], "too low cut"[126], "accepted various gifts from him, including Tiffany gold earrings

118 Feltner v. Partyka, 945 F. Supp. 1188 (N.D. Ind., Oct. 8, 1996); Feltner v. Title Search Co., (7th Cir., Sept. 2, 1998)

119 Sorrells v. Hickman, 2006 U.S. Dist. LEXIS 99362, (W.D. Ark., June 8, 2006)

120 O'Dell v. Trans World Entm't Corp., 153 F. Supp. 2d 378 (S.D.N.Y., June 29, 2001)

121 Mack on behalf of Wesley v. Sullivan, 813 F. Supp. 760 (D. Kan., Jan. 29, 1993)

122 Ammons v. State Dep't of Soc. & Health Servs., 648 F.3d 1020; (9th Cir , Wash., Aug. 17, 2011)

123 United States v. Kelley, 2006 U.S. Dist. LEXIS 88350 (E.D. Ark., Dec. 5, 2006)

124 A&H Sportswear Co. v. Victoria's Secret Stores, Inc., 926 F. Supp. 1233 (E.D.Pa., May 24, 1996)

125 Victoria's Secret Stores v. Artco Equip. Co., 194 F. Supp. 2d 704 (S.D. Ohio, March 27, 2002)

126 Seats v. Kaskaskia College Cmty. College Dist. # 501, 2008 U.S. Dist. LEXIS 100944 (S.D. Ill., Dec. 15, 2008)

on Valentine's Day, and a cell phone, calculator, and Palm Pilot"[127], "gave him back massages"[128], "purchased her a membership in a gym"[129], "a 12-gauge shotgun, was only a Valentine's Day gift for a co-defendant"[130]

"Valentine's Day greeting"[131], "love poem"[132], "To My Wife on Valentine's Day,"[133] "handwritten letter"[134], "printed endearments"[135], "Valentine's Day poem"[136],

127 Bogdan v. N.Y. City Transit Auth., 2005 U.S. Dist. LEXIS 9317 (S.D.N.Y., May 17, 2005).

128 Escue v. N. Okla. College, 450 F.3d 1146; (10th Cir., June 14, 2006)

129 Blanco v. Brogan, 2007 U.S. Dist. LEXIS 86890 (S.D.N.Y., Nov. 21, 2007)

130 United States v. Ferryman, 444 F.3d 1183 (9th Cir., Jan. 25, 2006)

131 Kennedy v. McCarty, 778 F. Supp. 1465 (S.D. Ind., Nov. 25, 1991); United States v. Rich, 2000 U.S. App. LEXIS 15807 (6th Cir., June 29, 2000); Wilton Indus. v. United States, 31 C.I.T. 863; 493 F. Supp. 2d 1294 (June 11, 2007); Kennedy v. Dickenson, 2009 U.S. Dist. LEXIS 83015, (C.D. Cal., Sept. 10, 2009)

132 Guaraldi v. Cunningham, 819 F.2d 15 (1st Cir., May 29, 1987)

133 Grove v. United States, 170 F. Supp. 176 (E.D. Va., Feb. 10, 1959)

134 United States v. Andreozzi, 60 M.J. 727 (C.A.A.F., Nov. 4, 2004)

135 Magill v. Precision Sys. Mfg., 2006 U.S. Dist. LEXIS 16923 (N.D.N.Y., Feb. 27, 2006)

"Valentine's Day card, a photograph, and a book of poetry"[137], "card from his girlfriend"[138], "The card is signed 'Love, Daddy.' "[139], "he sent her a Valentine's Day card signed 'Love, John.' "[140],

"card which stated 'I can't imagine loving you more than I do today . . . but tomorrow I will. HAPPY VALENTINE'S DAY, SWEETHEART.' "[141], "card telling her how much he loved her"[142], "remembered her with cards and gifts", "card and candy"[143]

---

136 Guaraldi v. Cunningham, 819 F.2d 15 (1st Cir., May 29, 1987)

137 O'Connor v. Ortega, 480 U.S. 709 (March 31, 1987)

138 Webster v. Fischer, 694 F. Supp. 2d 163 (N.D.N.Y., Feb. 22, 2010)

139 Wendorf v. Metropolitan Life Ins. Co., 1988 U.S. Dist. LEXIS 9214 (E.D.N.Y., Aug. 5, 1988)

140 Smith v. Ford, 1996 U.S. Dist. LEXIS 22942 (W.D. Tenn., Oct. 15, 1996)

141 Johnson v. Brown, 1998 U.S. Dist. LEXIS 12689 (N.D. Ill., Aug. 10, 1998); Johnson v. West, 218 F.3d 725 (7th Cir., July 5, 2000)

142 Jones v. Swanson, 341 F.3d 723 (8th Cir., Sept. 3, 2003)

143 Pines v. Bd. of Regents of the Univ. of Mich, 2012 U.S. Dist. LEXIS 13856 (E.D. Mich., Feb. 6, 2012,)

"Valentine's Day Dance"[144], "drove twenty-five miles to a Valentine's Day party"[145], "It being Valentine's Day, plaintiffs wanted to dine"[146], "had a hot date"[147], "dinner"[148], "lunch meeting"[149], "she and her husband were attending an early evening St. Valentine's Day cocktail party"[150],

144 Student Coalition for Peace v. Lower Merion School Dist., 596 F. Supp. 169 (E.D. Pa., Sept. 28, 1984); Doe v. Taylor Indep. Sch. Dist., 975 F.2d 137 (5th Cir., Oct. 2, 1992); Doe v. Taylor Indep. Sch. Dist., 15 F.3d 443 (5th Cir., March 3, 1994); Ings-Ray v. Sch. Dist. of Phila., 2003 U.S. Dist. LEXIS 7683 (E.D. Pa., April 30, 2003); Taylor v. Bradshaw, 2006 U.S. Dist. LEXIS 97381 (S.D. Ohio, July 14, 2006); Salter v. McNesby, 2007 U.S. Dist. LEXIS 62712 (N.D. Fla, Aug. 24, 2007); Burch v. Millas, 663 F. Supp. 2d 151 (W.D.N.Y., Aug. 14, 2009); Register v. Colvin, 944 F. Supp. 2d 1161 (N.D. Fla., May 10, 2013)

145 Cooper v. Blevins, 1991 U.S. Dist. LEXIS 2592 (E.D. Pa., March 1, 1991); United States v. Cassavetes, 2000 U.S. App. LEXIS 33455 (10th Cir., Dec. 21, 2000); Goulart v. Meadows, 345 F.3d 239 (4th Cir., Sept. 26, 2003); Pounds v. Katy Indep. Sch. Dist., 517 F. Supp. 2d 901 (S.D. Tex., Sept. 24, 2007); Gates v. Tex. Dep't of Protective & Regulatory Servs., 537 F.3d 404 (5th Cir, July 28, 2008);

Miller v. Knowles, 2008 U.S. Dist. LEXIS 77109 (E.D. Cal., Sept. 26, 2008); Turcio v. Ricci, 2010 U.S. Dist. LEXIS 52222 (D.N.J., May 26, 2010)

146 Mendez v. Pizza Hut of Am., Inc., 2002 U.S. Dist. LEXIS 19231 (N.D. Ill., Oct. 3, 2002)

147 Wyrick v. City of Chi., 2003 U.S. Dist. LEXIS 13821, (N.D. Ill., Aug. 7, 2003)

148 Doe v. Taylor Indep. Sch. Dist., 975 F.2d 137 (5th Cir., Oct. 2, 1992, Decided); Doe v. Taylor Indep. Sch. Dist., 15 F.3d 443 (5th Cir., March 3, 1994); Ings-Ray v. Sch. Dist. of Phila., 2003 U.S. Dist. LEXIS 7683 (E.D.P.A., May 1, 2003); Taylor v. Bradshaw, 2006 U.S. Dist. LEXIS 9738 (S.D. Ohio, July 14, 2006); Salter v. McNesby, 2007 U.S. Dist. LEXIS 62712 (N.D. Fla., Aug. 24, 2007); Burch v. Millas, 663 F. Supp. 2d 151 (W.D.N.Y, Aug. 14, 2009)

149 United States v. Cantrell, 2008 U.S. Dist. LEXIS 95236 (N.D. Ind., Nov. 20, 2008) Decision reached on appeal by United States v. Cantrell, 2010 U.S. App. LEXIS 17021 (7th Cir. Ind., Aug. 11, 2010)

"out to dinner for Valentine's Day"[151], "A Valentine Day's dance was held for students at the Gym."[152] "St. Valentine's Day dance, which was held at the Hadji Shrine Temple"[153], "the post office was being decorated for Valentine's Day, and coffee and cookies were being served"[154], "party for homeschooled students"[155], "After a school-sponsored Valentine's Day dance, Jane Doe spent the night"[156].

"romantically involved"[157], "romantic tryst"[158], "couple's Valentine's Day celebrations"[159], "romantic evening"[160],

150 Morton v. United States, 233 F. Supp. 1011 (E.D.N.C., Sept. 18, 1964)

151 Schmidt v. Scribner, 2005 U.S. Dist. LEXIS 25699 (E.D. Cal., Oct. 27, 2005)

152 Student Coalition for Peace v. Lower Merion School Dist., 596 F. Supp. 169 (E.D.Pa., Sept. 28, 1984)

153 Salter v. McNesby, 2007 U.S. Dist. LEXIS 62712 (N.D. Fla., Aug. 24, 2007)

154 Robinson v. United States Postal Serv., 1995 U.S. Dist. LEXIS 14452 (E.D. Pa., Sept. 27, 1995)

155 Goulart v. Meadows, 345 F.3d 239 (4th Cir., Sept. 26, 2003)

156 Doe v. Taylor Indep. Sch. Dist., 975 F.2d 137 (5th Cir., Oct. 2, 1992)

157 United States v. Cardreon, 52 M.J. 213 (C.A.A.F., Dec. 9, 1999)

"expressions of love and affection"[161],
"nonsexual advances"[162],
"alleged sexual encounter"[163],
"lived with his girlfriend"[164], "nude"[165],
"living together in an intimate homosexual relationship"[166], "engaged to be married"[167],
"every man needs a wife"[168],
"love you very much"[169],

---

158 United States v. Shipe, 2008 U.S. Dist. LEXIS 59614 (E.D. Tenn,, May 28, 2008) Adopted by, Motion denied by United States v. Shipe, 2008 U.S. Dist. LEXIS 59610 (E.D. Tenn., July 22, 2008)

159 Gilbert v. New Line Prods., 2010 U.S. Dist. LEXIS 141516 (C.D. Cal., Aug. 13, 2010)

160 Hurth v. Campbell, 2009 U.S. Dist. LEXIS 115434, (E.D. Cal, Dec. 11, 2009)

161 Florey v. Sioux Falls School Dist., 619 F.2d 1311 (8th Cir., April 22, 1980)

162 Cram v. Lamson & Sessions Co., 49 F.3d 466 (8th Cir. , March 15, 1995)

163 Terrell v. King, 2011 U.S. Dist. LEXIS 85172 (S.D. Miss., July 8, 2011) Writ of habeas corpus dismissed, Certificate of appealability denied Terrell v. King, 2011 U.S. Dist. LEXIS 85655 (S.D. Miss., Aug. 2, 2011)

164 Woolever v. Lopez, 2011 U.S. Dist. LEXIS 85393 (E.D. Cal., Aug. 3, 2011)

165 Nicely v. Lewis, 2008 U.S. Dist. LEXIS 24648 (E.D. Tenn., March 27, 2008); Covenant Media of Ill., L.L.C. v. City of Des Plaines, Ill., 2009 U.S. Dist. LEXIS 66574, (N.D. Ill., July 31, 2009); Doe v. Crane, 2010 U.S. Dist. LEXIS 105518 (W.D. Mo., Oct. 4, 2010)

166 Wiswall v. Tanner, 145 B.R. 672 (W.D. Wash., Sept. 30, 1992)

167 United States v. Cardreon, 52 M.J. 213 (C.A.A.F., Dec. 9, 1999)

168 Stafford v. Missouri, 835 F. Supp. 1136 (W.D. Miss., Oct. 13, 1993)

169 Mack on behalf of Wesley v. Sullivan, 813 F. Supp. 760 (D. Kan., Jan. 29, 1993)

"personal ad"[170] ,
"classified Valentine's Day
advertisement"[171],
"message in the local newspaper"[172],
"notes from a female"[173],
 "flurry of e-mails"[174],
"became 'pen-pals'"[175],
"weekly telephone conversation"[176],
"illegal communication"[177],
"pimp games"[178]

"This Valentine's Day it's easy to become
entangled in an affair"[179],

---

170 Schlichter v. Limerick Twp., 2006 U.S. Dist. LEXIS 57399, (E.D. Pa., Aug. 15, 2006).

171 Gilliam v. USD #244 Sch. Dist., 397 F. Supp. 2d 1282 (D. Kan., Oct. 27, 2005)

172 Schlichter v. Limerick Twp., 2005 U.S. Dist. LEXIS 7287 (E.D. Pa., April 26, 2005); Willson v. Yerke, 2011 U.S. Dist. LEXIS 8739 (M.D. Pa., Jan. 31, 2011)

173 Reed v. Buckeye Fire Equip. Co., 422 F. Supp. 2d 570 (W.D.N.C., March 22, 2006)

174 Marangos v. Flarion Techs., Inc., 264 Fed. Appx. 176; (3d Cir., Feb. 12, 2008

175 United States v. Winckelmann, 70 M.J. 403 (C.A.A.F.,Dec. 12, 2011)

176 Budget Rent-A-Car Sys. v. Chappell, 304 F. Supp. 2d 639 (E.D. Pa., Feb. 2, 2004)

177 Ashker v. Schwarzenegger, 2009 U.S. Dist. LEXIS 25092 (N.D. Cal., March 25, 2009,)

178 Kokkinis v. Ivkovich, 185 F.3d 840 (7th Cir., July 26, 1999)

179 Rogers v. Grimaldi, 695 F. Supp. 112 (S.D.N.Y., Aug. 8, 1988)

"five-star hotel for the weekend"[180], "motel"[181], "condoms and key card"[182], "He suggested intercourse, but she refused"[183], "female co-worker, stated, 'I was thinking of you on Valentines Day. I wouldn't mind at all if you wanted to sneak'"[184], "extra-marital affair"[185],

"You're so gosh-darned huggable"[186], "a hug each day"[187], "daily 'friendly' hug"[188], "I just want to least hug my wife for Valentine's Day and that's it."[189]

---

180 Gagliardi v. Comm'r, T.C. Memo 2008-10 (Jan. 24, 2008)

181 Allen v. Senkowski, 178 F. Supp. 2d 318 (E.D.N.Y.., Dec. 26, 2001) Affirmed by Allen v. Senkowski, 2004 U.S. App. LEXIS 8696 (2d Cir. N.Y., May 3, 2004)

182 Schlichter v. Limerick Twp., 2006 U.S. Dist. LEXIS 57399 (E.D.Pa., Aug. 14, 2006)

183 Doe v. Taylor Indep. Sch. Dist., 975 F.2d 137 (5th Cir., Oct. 2, 1992)

184 United States v. Ardolf, 2010 U.S. Dist. LEXIS 91621 (D. Minn., Aug. 13, 2010)

185 Kroll v. White Lake Ambulance Auth., 2010 U.S. Dist. LEXIS 85404 (W.D. Mich., Aug. 19, 2010)

186 Magill v. Precision Sys. Mfg., 2006 U.S. Dist. LEXIS 16923 (N.D. N.Y., Feb. 27, 2006)

187 Troge v. J.C. Penney Co., 43 F. Supp. 2d 1343 (M.D. Fla., April 14, 1999)

188 Troge v. J.C. Penney Co., 43 F. Supp. 2d 1343 (M.D. Fla., April 14, 1999)

"frequently discussing 'his sex life' with Balas, giving her Valentine's Day candy, stating a desire to hug her"[190], "sexual overtures toward her"[191], "sexually suggestive"[192], "ensuing sexual activity"[193], "they had intercourse over the Valentine's Day weekend"[194], "You were fucking your husband for Valentine's Day"[195], "that she would be giving her husband 'p****' for Valentine's Day, 'all the p****he wants' "[196] "in America, you kiss and date"[197],

189 Young v. Hedgpeth, 2009 U.S. Dist. LEXIS 68513 (C.D. Cal., July 6, 2009)

190 Balas v. Huntington Ingalls Indus., 2011 U.S. Dist. LEXIS 110138 (E.D. Va., Sept. 26, 2011)

191 Smith v. Ford, U.S. Dist. LEXIS 22942 (W.D. Tenn., Oct. 15, 1996)

192 EEOC v. Love's Travel Stops & Country Stores, Inc., 677 F. Supp. 2d 1176 (D. Ariz., Dec. 30, 2009)

193 United States v. Andreozzi, 60 M.J. 727; 2004 (C.C.A., Nov. 2004)

194 Chapman v. Felkner, 2009 U.S. Dist. LEXIS 126926 (C.D. Cal., Dec. 17, 2009)

195 Case v. Midwestern Sports Med. & Orthopaedic Surgical Specialists, 2005 U.S. Dist. LEXIS 33652 (N.D. Ill., Dec. 15, 2005)

196 Walker v. SBC Servs., 375 F. Supp. 2d 524 (N.D. Tex., June 2, 2005)

197 Adil Lahrichi v. Lumera Corp., 2006 U.S. Dist. LEXIS 18556 (W.D. Wash., March 2, 2006)

"received by mail a large red Valentine card reading, 'On Valentine's Day, remember-- candy is dandy...but sex won't rot your teeth!' "[198],

"French is the language of love"[199]
"asked 'can I give you a kiss?' while offering her chocolate Hershey kisses"[200]
"they call me walking chocolate."[201]

"champagne"[202], "bottle of gin"[203], "drank more than ten but less than twenty twelve ounce cups of beer"[204],

---

198 Pucci v. USAIR, 940 F. Supp. 305 (M.D. Fla., Sept. 27, 1996)

199 Bruno v. Monroe County, 2009 U.S. Dist. LEXIS 84364 (S.D. Fla., Aug. 31, 2009)

200 Lisiecki v. Racine County, 2005 U.S. Dist. LEXIS 40145 (E.D. Wisc., Sept. 19, 2005)

201 Mitchell v. City of Pittsburgh, 2014 U.S. Dist. LEXIS 6119 (W.D. Pa., Jan. 17, 2014)

202 Soliman v. Deutsche Bank AG, 2004 U.S. Dist. LEXIS 9087 (S.D.N.Y., May 19, 2004)

203 McCaskill v. ConAgra Foods, Inc., 296 F. Supp. 2d 1311 (M.D. Ala., Dec. 22, 2003,)

204 Cooper v. Blevins, 1991 U.S. Dist. LEXIS 2592 (E.D.Pa., March 1, 1991)

"inhaling methamphetamine at a Valentine's Day party in 1999"[205], "furnishing methamphetamine to Lucy at the Valentine's Day party"[206], "One of the packages containing the cocaine had a Valentine's Day card attached"[207]

"gifts triggered an emotional strain"[208], "emotions, however, proved fickle"[209], "he misunderstood her reaction to his Valentine's Day present"[210], "She was 'a little' surprised"[211], "reduced to tears because plaintiff refused to accept a Valentine's Day gift."[212],

205 United States v. Cassavetes,. 2000 U.S. App. LEXIS 33455 (10th Cir., Colo., Dec. 21, 2000,)

206 Miller v. Knowles, 2008 U.S. Dist. LEXIS 77109 (E.D. Cal., Sept. 26, 2008)

207 United States v. Walker, 1996 U.S. App. LEXIS 33318 (10th Cir, Dec. 20, 1996) Certiorari Denied April 21, 1997, Reported at: 1997 U.S. LEXIS 2622.

208 Porchia v. Cohen, 1999 U.S. Dist. LEXIS 8239 (E.D. Pa., June 3, 1999)

209 Jones v. Swanson, 341 F.3d 723 (8th Cir., Sept. 3, 2003) Motion denied by,

210 Burleson v. Kernan, 2007 U.S. Dist. LEXIS 86964 (N.D. Cal., , Nov. 15, 2007)

211 United States v. Freeman, 2011 U.S. App. LEXIS 25494 (10th Cir., Dec. 21, 2011)

212 Palmer v. Board of Education, 466 F. Supp. 600 (N.D. Ill. , Jan. 31, 1979)

"asked him whether he had gotten his wife a Valentine's Day card, he responded that he had not but he should"[213],

"when the employee asked if he received a Valentine's day card, he said no, but that he should have"[214],

"he threw the Valentine's Day card away without reading it,"[215],

"he brought her Valentine's Day cookies, which she threw away"[216],

"he became extremely upset as a result of the Valentine's Day gift"[217],

"and the engagement were 'off and on'"[218]

213 Baskerville v. Culligan Int'l Co., 50 F.3d 428 (7th Cir., March 20, 1995)

214 Kendrick v. Country Club Hills Bd. of Educ. , 1998 U.S. Dist. LEXIS 11618 (N.D. Ill., July 23, 1998)

215 Pines v. Bd. of Regents of the Univ. of Mich., 2012 U.S. Dist. LEXIS 13856 (E.D. Mich., Feb. 6, 2012,)

216 Seats v. Kaskaskia College Cmty. College Dist. # 501, 2008 U.S. Dist. LEXIS 100944 (S.D. Ill., Dec. 15, 2008)

217 Feltner v. Partyka, 945 F. Supp. 1188 (N.D. Ind., Oct. 8, 1996)

218 Wilkens v. Newton-Embry, 2007 U.S. Dist. LEXIS 82250 (N.D. Okla., Nov. 5, 2007)

"After discovering Valentine Day cards from another man in his wife's purse, an argument"[219],
"she excluded him from participating"[220],
"go celebrate with the whore"[221],

"her Valentines Day had been 'ruined' when she encountered her former husband"[222],
"analogous to spending Valentine's Day with a spouse who has filed for divorce and professed love for someone else"[223],
"the couple got into an argument"[224],
"nearly lost your mind, had to get therapy"[225],

219 Wade v. Warden, Lebanon Corr. Inst., 2009 U.S. Dist. LEXIS 124237 (S.D. Ohio Nov. 10, 2009)

220 MacIntosh v. Davis, 2010 U.S. Dist. LEXIS 26500 (E.D. Mich., March 22, 2010)

221 Lopez v. Ercole, 2010 U.S. Dist. LEXIS 39274 (S.D.N.Y., April 21, 2010)

222 Snyder v. Millersville Univ., 2008 U.S. Dist. LEXIS 97943 (E.D.Pa., Dec. 3, 2008,)

223 Brotherson v. Prof'l Basketball Club, L.L.C., 2008 U.S. Dist. LEXIS 118029 (W.D. Wash., April 14, 2008) quoting Plaintiff argument.

224 Woolever v. Lopez, 2011 U.S. Dist. LEXIS 85393 (E.D. Cal., Aug. 2, 2011)

225 United States v. Gary, 18 F.3d 1123 (4th Cir., Feb. 28, 1994)

"depression continued throughout February"[226], "sleepless night"[227], "becoming more nervous"[228], "captivity"[229], "suicide"[230], "divorce settlement"[231], "divorce decree"[232], "lonely road"[233], "objectionable behavior"[234], "especially inappropriate"[235], "hostile work environment"[236], "abusive and vulgar language"[237],

226 Mason v. Smithkline Beecham Corp., 596 F.3d 387 (7th Cir., Feb. 23, 2010)

227 Galeski v. City of Dearborn, 690 F. Supp. 2d 603 (E.D. Mich., Jan. 27, 2010)

228 United States v. Kelley, 2006 U.S. Dist. LEXIS 88350 (E.D. Ark., Jan. 18, 2007)

229 Levin v. Islamic Republic of Iran, 529 F. Supp. 2d 1 (D.D.C., Dec. 31, 2007)

230 Mason v. Smithkline Beecham Corp. 596 F.3d 387 (7th Cir., Feb. 23, 2010); subsequent proceeding Mason v. Smithkline Beecham Corp., 2010 U.S. Dist. LEXIS 67293 (C.D. Ill., July 2, 2010)

231 Carlisle v. Carlisle (In re Carlisle), 205 B.R. 812 (Bankr., W.D. La., March 10, 1997)

232 Renfrow v. Draper, 232 F.3d 688 (9th Cir., Nov. 14, 2000)

233 Medus v. Federal Kemper Life Assur. Co., 1997 U.S. Dist. LEXIS 12015 (E.D. La., Aug. 4, 1997)

234 Naylor v. City of Bowie, 78 F. Supp. 2d 469 (D.Md., Dec. 9, 1999)

235 Snyder v. Millersville Univ., 2008 U.S. Dist. LEXIS 97943 (E.D. Pa., Dec. 3, 2008)

236 Schlichter v. Limerick Twp., , 2005 U.S. Dist. LEXIS 7287 (E.D. Pa., April 26, 2005,)

237 Verrinder v. Rite Aid Corp., 2007 U.S. Dist. LEXIS 90931 (W.D. Va., Dec. 11, 2007)

"ridiculed and humiliated"[238],
"humiliated, ignored"[239],

"request to leave her alone"[240],
"stalking incidents"[241],
"daily harassment"[242],
"Johnson never gave Williams permission to touch her"[243],
"Gallagher involved a claim of sexual harassment in which the defendant allegedly invited plaintiff to sit on his lap, gave her inappropriate Valentine's Day gifts, told her that 'she brought out feelings that he had not had since he was sixteen'"[244],

---

238 Ashok v. Barnhart, 289 F. Supp. 2d 305 (E.D.N.Y., Oct. 30, 2003)

239 Feltner v. Title Search Co., 1998 U.S. App. LEXIS 21691 (7th Cir., Sept. 2, 1998)

240 Aaseby v. Longo, 2010 U.S. Dist. LEXIS 68649 (D. Idaho, July 9, 2010)

241 Estate of Macias v. Ihde, 219 F.3d 1018 (9th Cir. Cal., July 20, 2000)

242 Feltner v. Title Search Co., 1998 U.S. App. LEXIS 21691 (7th Cir., Sept. 2, 1998)

243 Johnson v. Brown, 1998 U.S. Dist. LEXIS 12689 (N.D. Ill., Aug. 10, 1998)

244 Leonard v. Pepsico, Inc., 88 F. Supp. 2d 116 (S.D.N.Y., Aug. 5, 1999) citing Gallagher v. Delaney, 139 F.3d 338 (2d Cir. 1998)

"sit with a friend on a beautiful Valentine's Day night, and suddenly become prey to brutal predators"[245],

"his creation of an abusive and hostile environment"[246], "frustration with Plaintiff hit its boiling point"[247], "violating the terms of the temporary restraining order"[248],

"deadbeat dads"[249],

"a Valentine's day roundup"[250],

"generalized roundup of suspects, timed to coincide with Valentine's Day posed significant risks of harm to innocent reputations"[251].

---

245 United States v. Queensborough, 227 F.3d 149 (3d Cir., Sept. 15, 2000)

246 Feltner v. Partyka, 945 F. Supp. 1188 (N.D. Ind., Oct. 8, 1996)

247 Habe v. 333 Bayville Ave. Rest. Corp., 2012 U.S. Dist. LEXIS 4367 (E.D.N.Y., Jan. 12, 2012)

248 Estate of Macias v. Ihde, 219 F.3d 1018 (9th Cir, July 20, 2000);

249 Cannon v. Montgomery County, (1998 U.S. Dist. LEXIS 9502 (E.D. Pa., June 29, 1998)

250 Cannon v. Montgomery County, (1998 U.S. Dist. LEXIS 9502 (E.D. Pa., June 29, 1998)

251 Trusik v. Montgomery County, 1998 U.S. Dist. LEXIS 5935 (E.D. Pa., April 27, 1998)

"an obscene Valentine Day's card, addressed to 'Cunt' on her toolbox,"[252],

"that he had given her a Valentine's Day card picturing a duck and noting, 'Wish me a Happy Valentine's Day . . . or the duck is going to die,'"[253]

"the conspiracy ended with arrests on Valentine's Day"[254], "referring to the day of the crime"[255],

"drug offense"[256], "sexual batteries"[257], "larceny of a Valentine's Day card and $ 10.00 in U.S. currency"[258],

252 Carr v. Allison Gas Turbine Div., Gen. Motors Corp., 32 F.3d 1007 (7th Cir., July 26, 1994); Washington v. Board of Trustees of Cmty. College Dist. 509, 2001 U.S. Dist. LEXIS 442 (N.D. Ill., Jan. 18, 2001); Lisiecki v. Racine County, 2005 U.S. Dist. LEXIS 40145 (E.D. Wis., Sept. 19, 2005)

253 Bruce v. Potter, 2010 U.S. Dist. LEXIS 19954 (S.D. Ohio, March 5, 2010)

254 United States v. Craddock, 1992 U.S. Dist. LEXIS 3772 (E.D. Pa., March 24, 1992)

255 Trice v. Ward, 196 F.3d 1151 (10th Cir. Colo., Nov. 15, 1999)

256 Perez v. Thaler, 2011 U.S. Dist. LEXIS 117767 (S.D. Tex., Feb. 17, 2011)

257 Sharpe v. McDonough, 2006 U.S. Dist. LEXIS 71030, (N.D. Fla., June 15, 2006)

258 United States v. Nichols, 1995 CCA LEXIS 460 (Sept. 12, 1995)

"had stolen the VCR he had given her for Valentine's Day and she wanted it back"[259], "assault on Arnold's estranged wife Jennifer which took place on Valentine's Day"[260],

"personal property seized at the time of plaintiff's arrest, the Valentine's Day card"[261], "the seizure of the photograph, Valentine's Day card and book of poems were relevant to prove a pattern of sexual harassment"[262],

"killed by a random"[263],
"shot in the back"[264],
"shot dead on a street"[265].

259 Walker v. Cain, 2006 U.S. Dist. LEXIS 60113 (W.D. La., June 20, 2006)

260 Arnold v. Cockrell, 2002 U.S. Dist. LEXIS 12070, (N.D. Tex., July 2, 2002,)

261 Bonilla v. United States, 2008 U.S. Dist. LEXIS 70487 (E.D.N.Y, Sept. 3, 2008)/

262 Ortega v. O'Connor, 1996 U.S. Dist. LEXIS 4788 (N.D. Cal., March 12, 1996)

263 Kendall v. Vill. of Maywood, 2009 U.S. Dist. LEXIS 30917 (N.D. Ill., April 9, 2009)

264 Randle v. Jackson, Case Number: 544 F. Supp. 2d 619 (E.D. Mich,, March 31, 2008)

"St. Valentine's Day Massacre"[266],
"Valentine's day slaughter"[267],
"Valentine's Day prank"[268],
"Valentine's Day agreement"[269].

"The PNG army mounted an attack on February 14, 1990 - the St. Valentine's Day massacre - in which many civilians, including a Uniting Church pastor, were killed. Plaintiffs contend that, in response to this massacre, the Bougainville Revolutionary Army ('BRA') consolidated,

265 United States v. Hawkins, 380 F. Supp. 2d 143 (E.D.N.Y., Aug. 8, 2005) Affirmed by United States v. Hawkins, 228 Fed. Appx. 107, 2007 U.S. App. LEXIS 9932 (2d Cir. N.Y., Apr. 30, 2007)

266 Beauharnais v. Pittsburgh Courier Publishing Co., 243 F.2d 705 (7th Cir., April 19, 1957); United States v. Birrell, 286 F. Supp. 869 (S.D.N.Y., May 28, 1968); Herbert v. Lando, 73 F.R.D. 387 (S.D.N.Y., Jan. 4, 1977); Herbert v. Lando, 568 F.2d 974 (2d Cir., Nov. 7, 1977); Herbert v. Lando, 596 F. Supp. 1178 (S.D.N.Y., Oct. 11, 1984) Eclipse Enters. v. Gulotta, 942 F. Supp. 801 (E.D.N.Y., Sept. 26, 1996); Sarei v. Rio Tinto Plc, 221 F. Supp. 2d 1116 (C.D. Cal., July 11, 2002); Verrinder v. Rite Aid Corp., 2007 U.S. Dist. LEXIS 90931 (W.D. Va., Dec. 11, 2007); Sarei v. Rio Tinto, 550 F.3d 822 (9th Cir., Oct. 11, 2007); Perez v. Thaler, 2011 U.S. Dist. LEXIS 117767 (S.D. Tex., Feb. 17, 2011)

267 United States v. Birrell, 286 F. Supp. 869 (S.D.N.Y., May 28, 1968)

268 Priest v. Rotary, 634 F. Supp. 571 (N.D. Cal., Feb. 12, 1986)

269 Conrail v. Brotherhood of Maintenance of Way Employees, 781 F. Supp. 360 (E.D. Pa., Dec. 23, 1991)

Bougainvilleans called for secession from PNG, and 'the struggle to close the mine became a struggle for independence' that continued for almost a decade."[270]

"portraits of individuals, such as Al Capone and Eliot Ness, and historical events, such as the St. Valentine's Day Massacre with brief descriptions of each"[271],

"Valentine's Day anti-war artwork using nude individuals on a beach"[272],
"Viet Nam"[273],
"Valentine's Day rally at the state capitol to 'Stop the War on Poor Children'"[274],

270 Sarei v. Rio Tinto Plc, 221 F. Supp. 2d 1116 (C.D. Cal., July 9, 2002)

271 Eclipse Enters. v. Gulotta, 942 F. Supp. 801 (E.D.N.Y., Sept. 26, 1996)

272 Covenant Media of Ill., L.L.C. v. City of Des Plaines, Ill., 2009 U.S. Dist. LEXIS 66574, (N.D. Ill,. July 31, 2009)

273 Herbert v. Lando, 73 F.R.D. 387 (S.D.N.Y., Jan. 4, 1977)

274 Families Achieving Independence & Respect v. Nebraska Dep't of Social Servs., 91 F.3d 1076 (8th Cir., July 31, 1996)

"hospitalized"[275],
"Hospice inpatient unit"[276],

"diagnosed with squamous cell carcinoma. His penis was amputated on Valentines Day, 2007"[277]

"wearing silk heart shaped boxers in jail on Valentine's Day ... overheard an inmate call out, 'Oh, it's Valentine's Day, bring him here. He'd make a good girlfriend' "[278].

"dreamed"[279], "wished"[280], "kissed"[281], "celebrated"[282], "escalated"[283], "horses"[284],

275 Randle v. Jackson, 544 F. Supp. 2d 619 (E.D. Mich., March 31, 2008)

276 Metropolitan Life Ins. Co. v. Yeary, 1998 U.S. Dist. LEXIS 22835 (N.D. Ohio, Feb. 6, 1998)

277 Castaneda v. United States, 538 F. Supp. 2d 1279 (C.D. Cal., March 11, 2008)

278 United States v. Lanham, 617 F.3d 873 (6th Cir., Aug. 24, 2010)

279 Dintelman v. United States, 2012 U.S. Dist. LEXIS 13032 (E.D. Ark., Feb. 3, 2012)

280 Hirschfeld v. New Mexico Corrections Dep't, 916 F.2d 572 (10th Cir., Oct. 12, 1990)

281 Hirschfeld v. New Mexico Corrections Dep't, 916 F.2d 572 (10th Cir., Oct. 12, 1990)

282 United States v. Shaw, 560 F.3d 1230 (11th Cir., March 3, 2009)

"cattle haulers"[285], "crop loan"[286],
"silver revolver"[287], "clean the carpets"[288],

"red and white headbands"[289],
"community based instruction"[290],

"biology class"[291], "Ice Capades"[292],
"a pizza delivery boy"[293],
"his Elvis impression"[294],
"Dancing Cupid"[295],

---

283 Feltner v. Title Search Co., 1998 U.S. App. LEXIS 21691 (7th Cir., Sept. 2, 1998,); Mehringer v. Vill. of Bloomingdale, 2003 U.S. Dist. LEXIS 11040 (N.D. Ill., June 26, 2003)

284 Sheppard v. United States, 176 Ct. Cl. 244; 361 F.2d 972 (June 10, 1966)

285 Garcia-Quiroz v. United States, 2009 U.S. Dist. LEXIS 42765 (W.D. Tex., May 20, 2009)

286 Luker v. Eubanks (In re Eubanks), 444 B.R. 415 (E.D. Ark., Dec. 29, 2010)

287 Ogle v. Johnson, 696 F. Supp. 2d 1345 (S.D. Ga., June 29, 2009)

288 Wilkins v. Strickland, 2009 U.S. Dist. LEXIS 11373 (E.D. Cal., Feb. 3, 2009)

289 Litvinov v. Holder, 605 F.3d 548 (8th Cir., May 20, 2010)

290 D.B. v. Ocean Twp. Bd. of Educ., 1997 U.S. Dist. LEXIS 20395 (D.N.J., Nov. 21, 1997)

291 Doe v. Taylor Indep. Sch. Dist., 15 F.3d 443 (5th Cir., March 3, 1994)

292 Bostic v. United States Capitol Police, 644 F. Supp. 2d 106 (D.D.C. Aug. 6, 2009)

293 Miller v. Dees, 1999 U.S. Dist. LEXIS 17536 (S.D Ala., Sept. 9, 1999)

294 Hirschfeld v. New Mexico Corrections Dep't, 916 F.2d 572 (10th Cir., Oct. 12, 1990)

295 Wilton Indus. v. United States, 31 C.I.T. 863; 493 F. Supp. 2d 1294 (June 11, 2007)

"the generalized idea of a cupid's-arrow"[296],

"this policy does not stop Cupid's arrow from striking"[297].

"Happy Valentine's Day!"[298]

296 Bonazoli v. R.S.V.P. Int'l, Inc., 353 F. Supp. 2d 218 (D.R.I., Jan. 18, 2005)

297 Ellis v. UPS, Inc., 523 F.3d 823 (7th Cir., April 29, 2008)

298 Wendorf v. Metropolitan Life Ins. Co., 1988 U.S. Dist. LEXIS 9214)E.D.N.Y., Aug. 5, 1988); Hirschfeld v. New Mexico Corrections Dep't, 916 F.2d 572 (10th Cir., Oct. 12, 1990); Johnson v. Brown, 1998 U.S. Dist. LEXIS 12689 (N.D. Ill., Aug. 6, 1998);Johnson v. West, 218 F.3d 725 (7th Cir., July 5, 2000); Wyrick v. City of Chi., 2003 U.S. Dist. LEXIS 13821 (N.D. Ill., Aug. 7, 2003); Bellamy v. Fritz, 129 Fed. Appx. 245 (6th Cir., April 26, 2005); Sharpe v. McDonough, 2006 U.S. Dist. LEXIS 71030 (N.D. Fla., June 15, 2006); Wilton Indus. v. United States, 31 C.I.T. 863; 493 F. Supp. 2d 1294 (C.I.T. June 11, 2007); United States v. Lunceford, (S.D. Ala., Aug. 12, 2009); Bruno v. Monroe County, 2009 U.S. Dist. LEXIS 84364 (S.D. Fla., Aug. 31, 2009); Bruce v. Potter, 2010 U.S. Dist. LEXIS 19954 (S.D. Ohio, March 5, 2010); Idy v. Holder, 674 F.3d 111 (1st Cir., March 23, 2012)

ABOUT THE EDITOR

Joshua Warren is an artist, educator, scientist,
practicing attorney, and doctoral student with an
interest in politics, language and creativity.

This book is part of a series entitled Law of the Horse.

currently available:
Werewolf in the Federal Courts
Red Herring in the Supreme Court
Mad Scientist in the Federal Courts
Cocker Spaniel in the Federal Courts
Dachshund in the Federal Courts
Zombie in the Federal Courts

coming soon:
Creativity in the Supreme Court
Ninja in the Federal Courts
and more...

Other artwork by Joshua Warren can be found at:
warrbo.com